# WORKFORCE RENEWAL

## Increasing the Quality and Quantity of Work

Bernard H. Petrina

# A FIFTY-MINUTE™ SERIES BOOK

**CRISP PUBLICATIONS, INC.**
Menlo Park, California

# WORKFORCE RENEWAL
## Increasing the Quality and Quantity of Work

**Bernard H. Petrina**

**CREDITS:**
Editor: **Christopher Carrigan**
Typesetting: **ExecuStaff**
Cover Design: **Barbara Ravizza**
Artwork: **Ralph Mapson**

Copyright © 1994 Crisp Publications, Inc.
Printed in the United States of America.

English language Crisp books are distributed worldwide. Our major international distributors include:

CANADA: Reid Publishing, Ltd., Box 69559—109 Thomas St., Oakville, Ontario Canada L6J 7R4. TEL: (416) 842-4428, FAX: (416) 842-9327

AUSTRALIA: Career Builders, P.O. Box 1051, Springwood, Brisbane, Queensland, Australia 4127. TEL: 841-1061, FAX: 841-1580

NEW ZEALAND: Career Builders, P.O. Box 571, Manurewa, Auckland, New Zealand. TEL: 266-5276, FAX: 266-4152

JAPAN: Phoenix Associates Co., Mizuho Bldg. 2-12-2, Kami Osaki, Shinagawa-Ku, Tokyo 141, Japan. TEL: 3-443-7231, FAX: 3-443-7640

Selected Crisp titles are also available in other languages. Contact International Rights Manager Suzanne Kelly at (415) 323-6100 for more information.

**Library of Congress Catalog Card Number 93-73205**
Petrina, Bernard H.
Workforce Renewal
ISBN 1-56052-270-4

This book is printed on recyclable paper with soy ink.

# ABOUT THIS BOOK

*Workforce Renewal* is not like most books. It has a unique "self-paced" format that encourages a reader to become personally involved. Designed to be "read with a pencil," there are exercises, activities, assessments and cases that invite participation.

This book is intended to serve as a guide for the organizations that have survived the turbulent 1980s. Involvement—Feedback—Intercommunications—Accountability, all the things at work in a healthy atmosphere, are examined and exercises are presented to help the reader through the seven-step renewal process.

*Workforce Renewal* can be used effectively in a number of ways. Here are some possibilities:

—**Individual Study.** Because the book is self-instructional, all that is needed is a quiet place, some time and a pencil. Completing the activities and exercises will provide valuable feedback, as well as practical ideas for improving your business.

—**Workshops and Seminars.** This book is ideal for use during, or as preassigned reading prior to, a workshop or seminar. With the basics in hand, the quality of participation will improve. More time can be spent practicing concept extensions and applications during the program.

—**College Programs.** Thanks to the format, brevity and low cost, this book is ideal for short courses and extension programs.

There are other possibilities that depend on the objectives of the user. One thing is certain: even after it has been read, this book will serve as excellent reference material that can be easily reviewed.

# ABOUT THE AUTHOR

Bernard Hugh Petrina, M.A. is the president of Executive Management Renewal Programs. He has been speaking about and leading individuals and companies to achieve change and renewal for over twenty years. His custom-designed, professional development programs and training resources in human relations, management, and sales and marketing are used by individuals and innovative companies, large and small, throughout the country.

If you want to communicate with Mr. Petrina, you can write to:

> Executive-Management Renewal Programs
> P.O. Box 6309
> Harrisburg, PA 17112
> Phone 1-800-535-3633

# PREFACE

Our society doesn't like change. In fact, we glorify stability and consistency, so the things that are happening in society are uncomfortable. We would prefer that nobody tamper with our little world. It is the proverbial cry of mothers to, "stay out of my kitchen," of fathers to, "stay away from my tools," and of teenagers to, "stay out of my room." But nobody seems to be listening. We are in each other's lives all the time.

The president and congress are making changes that affect us. Organizations and corporations are changing. The economics of the whole world is changing. But the most important changes are the ones that are happening in our company or organization and many of these changes seem beyond our control. We are in the midst of a high-tech revolution, yet some of us want to maintain a low-tech presence. One thing seems certain; doing nothing is no longer an option.

Renewal means "to make new again." It is not a return to the way things were, they're gone forever. It doesn't mean reinventing the wheel, somebody already did that. It means making things simpler, or making them better or finding something different that works better. It means achieving a new comfort level by making something new feel like something old because we are getting used to the new fit. It means a new level of maturity where we learn to jettison some attitudes and habits in excited exchange for new ones.

This book is itself part of the process of change from an earlier work, "Motivating People To Care" by Bernard Petrina. The exercises can be done individually or in a group setting. All of them have been thoroughly field tested and have proven to be useful.

> **Destiny is not a matter of chance, it is a matter of choice.**

We wish you well as you become involved in the process of renewal.

Bernard H. Petrina

# ACKNOWLEDGMENTS

Thousands of people helped me write this book over the past twenty years. Some were at all those seminars and conferences because they wanted to be there, and some were there because someone else wanted them to be there. At each program, I warned them that if they took the contents seriously the person who walked out of the room would be different than the person who walked in.

It has been most gratifying to read the feedback of appreciative participants who caught the spirit of renewal in those encounters.

I sincerely believe the same admonition holds true for you, the reader. If you take this material seriously, you too will experience renewal.

To all those folks, to you the reader, to Nancy my spouse and business partner, to Shirley my secretary, for all the creative energy that you have contributed, and finally to Mike Crisp and Phil Gerould of Crisp Publications, who encouraged me to do it, this book is humbly dedicated.

# CONTENTS

# INTRODUCTION

*"Today is not yesterday; we ourselves change; how can our
works and thoughts, if they are always to be the fittest, continue
always the same?"*

— Thomas Carlyle

Workforce renewal is a wise personal and business investment for those
who want to survive and grow. No matter the age or size of a company or
organization, changes in the workplace and the workforce require a periodic
renewal of the way we operate. Workplace education is an essential part of
renewal. Ignorance is not bliss but may cause arrogance. Poorly educated
workers assume that their limited scope of knowledge is the total sum of all
knowledge. They can become arrogant with coworkers or customers and
create an atmosphere of discord and stress. The more we learn, the more we
realize how much more there is to learn.

Einstein said he only used 15% of his brain—imagine where that leaves the
rest of us. Commentators who study the human mind say he probably used
a lot less than 1/10th of 1%—he had no idea how potent his mental capacity
really was and neither do we.

On-the-job education that instills or renews essential principles can have a
profound, positive effect on the atmosphere of the workplace and the
attitudes of coworkers.

---

### RENEWAL IS PROFESSIONAL DEVELOPMENT

Renewal:

- Helps workers learn new technology faster
- Increases worker morale and commitment
- Promotes better communications internally and externally
- Increases the quality and quantity of work
- Produces greater awareness of the importance of competitiveness
- Causes workers to develop greater trust and pride in their organization
- Reduces conflict and prejudice
- Enables workers to accept empowerment with greater self-confidence

---

# SECTION

# I

# What Is Workforce Renewal?

# WHAT IS RENEWAL?

Renewal means "to make new again." A renewal is a fresh start. Renewal is familiar to all of us: each year we renew our driver's license or renew an insurance policy.

The purpose of this book is to redefine our changing commitments and priorities within the scope of our jobs and careers.

Renewing the workforce means much more than renewing work contracts. It means redefining who we are and why we are part of an organization that is redefining why it exists.

Renewal cuts through the layers of policies, procedures and problems that slowly eat into an organization, stifling growth and creativity.

Renewal reevaluates what is important and what is not, taking an honest look at what we must do and what we should set aside. Renewal does not concentrate on short-term gain but on basic adjustments needed for long term results. To be complete, renewal takes a new look at our purpose, mission and plan, our whole perspective of involvement, and the interrelationships of every person in the enterprise.

## Characteristics of Renewal

There are three characteristics of a renewed person or organization.

1. **Ability to Cope with Change**

   > Renewal is not a retreat, it is an advance, a new start.

2. **Positive, Self-confident Attitudes**

   > You cannot advance in an environment of negativity or despair.

3. **Ability to Prioritize Goals, Objectives and Activities**

   > Renewal means doing what counts, not counting what you do.

Individuals or organizations fail when they do not have these characteristics.

# ELEMENTS OF THE RENEWAL PROCESS

Aristotle said that the beginning of philosophy is wonder. The beginning of renewal is an unsatisfcatory situation; unsatisfactory because it is uncomfortable, evil, degrading, harmful, or threatening our well being. The individual perceives a desirable reward if he or she changes the situation. The important point is that the reason we do things is more than one act, it is a process.

There are five elements that lead to renewal, which can occur over a period of time or instantly.

## ELEMENTS OF RENEWAL

1. FIND INSPIRATION
2. FUEL IMAGINATION
3. AWAKEN DESIRE
4. MAKE A DECISION
5. TAKE ACTION

## 1. FIND INSPIRATION

Inspiration animates the human spirit. Creativity and genius are explosions of activity ignited by the spark of inspiration. We sometimes expect the activity without creating the spark. But every worthwhile accomplishment begins with a dream, an idea, a vision. Inspiration causes a lump in the throat, a tear in the eye, a pounding of the heart. Without inspiration there is no motivation and little accomplishment.

## 2. FUEL IMAGINATION

The human mind is a dream machine. Imagination is the fuel that makes the dream machine work. Imagination creates alluring mental pictures that make the reality more and more attractive. This is the wish stage. Many inspirations die at this point or never make it to the next level because of doubt and lack of confidence. We start to listen to people who say ''it can't be done—it won't work.''

## 3. AWAKEN DESIRE

Desire converts wishes into wants. The vision in the mind is now seen as a real possibility and we believe. Desire gives us a new look, a way to get what we are imagining. Our dream machine says, ''You can have it if you want it,'' ''It can be done.''

## 4. MAKE A DECISION

Decision is based on believing we can get what we want, if we are willing to pay the price. Decision says, ''I am willing to pay the price because the pay-off is worth it.'' Decision focuses us on the ''how to.''

## 5. TAKE ACTION

Decision focuses us on the action necessary to achieve our goals. The attained result is the payoff. When the first four elements of the renewal process are completed and an action takes place, the action creates more inspiration. That is why an inventor who develops a successful device is further inspired and often creates a series of inventions. Entrepreneurs who succeed at an enterprise are often inspired to begin new ventures.

Renewal is a motivational process so powerful it has made poor people millionaires and the disabled world champions.

# ELEMENTS OF THE RENEWAL PROCESS (continued)

Suggested *Elements* that will PROMOTE or HINDER the renewal process.

| Elements that *Promote* Renewal | Elements that *Hinder* Renewal |
|---|---|
| • Openness | • Sarcasm |
| • Ability to withhold judgment | • Over reaction |
| • Belief in people | • Unwillingness to risk |
| • Ability to overlook minor digs | • Impatience |
| • A sense of humor | • Hidden agendas |
| **What other elements can PROMOTE RENEWAL in your organization?** | **What other elements can HINDER RENEWAL in your organization?** |
| | |

# THE OBJECTIVES OF RENEWAL

In order to renew an organization, there are three areas to explore.

### 1. Knowledge
### 2. Technique
### 3. Motivation

## KNOWLEDGE

Knowledge is the fuel of modern technology. Modern technology is a relative term. A crossbow was modern military technology in the Middle Ages—today it's the ICBM.

> *"State-of-the-art" is a phrase that implies change. It really means, the best we've got today to get the job done.*

What do we know now that we didn't know in the past? What are the limits of our knowledge? What skills do we need to be state-of-the-art? Knowledge carries with it a sense of priority and urgency that requires timely information to resolve current situations. Knowledge carries with it a sense of responsibility, obliging us to use our knowledge to develop our society and our people. The products and services we produce require knowledge of the marketplace, knowledge of lifestyles, knowledge of manufacturing, and knowledge of customer relations. Education thus becomes a key component for people and organizations who seek renewal.

As the state-of-the-art changes, the power source changes with it. The horse was our state-of-the-art power source for travel, agriculture, communications and war.

We experienced the great industrial revolution. The power source then became "manpower." Immigrants streamed into cities, factories, mines, mills and shops.

Now the power source has become "brain power." Knowledge is the real state-of-the-art in the Age of Information, but it's not what you've got that counts, it's what you do with what you've got.

# THE OBJECTIVES OF RENEWAL (continued)

Brain power devised ways to make mighty machines smaller and faster, doing more with less physical exertion. We moved from mechanics to electronics and now to photonics (lasers and fiber optics).

We sought instant response because we wanted more time for ourselves to do what we wanted rather than what we had to do. So we got instant information, instant copies, instant pictures, instant replay, instant food, and sometimes we needed instant relief.

Each advance had side effects and repercussions. When we went from horses to cars, buggy makers and blacksmiths lost jobs. Clearly new human awareness and adjustment is needed with each new step of technological change.

## TECHNIQUE

How we do what we do needs to be evaluated. Theory must be transformed into practical methods that work.

The 1940s was the beginning of the global economy as distinct from a national or even a local economy. Goods and services now cross not only rivers and mountains, but oceans and continents as well.

In today's service society, more than 80% of Americans are in occupations that service the market rather than produce basic products as was the case in the industrial society.

Techniques for dealing with change are based on our ability to understand what is happening, and to respond to what we learn with solutions to problems and innovative ideas to open new markets.

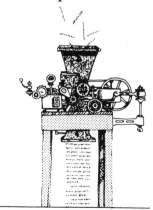

## MOTIVATION

**Two Kinds of Motivation: Inspirational and Educational.**

1. **Inspirational motivation** is the result of feelings, experienced when we are moved by ideas, sights or sounds. It may come from a speech, a sermon, a motivational tape or even by observing nature's grandeur. Our indescribable feelings can result in a poem, a great work of art, music, or a decision to accomplish some humanitarian deed. The ultimate inspirational motivation is to offer one's life for a cause. We see this on television every day as people all over the world march with signs, slogans and chants.

2. **Educational or achievement motivation** is the result of thinking and training. Training that excites us to make changes in the way we think is educational motivation.

   When we know we will be rewarded for doing certain activities and we want the reward, we can be motivated to perform those activities. This can happen whether we are trying to get the kids to clean up their room or trying to motivate a salesperson to increase his or her productivity. Educational motivation connects an activity with a reward.

   All renewal begins with personal renewal. You are a unique individual with unique abilities, talents, wants and desires. We become personally motivated when we are inspired by wants and wishes that create internal satisfaction.

# *My Motivators*

Number the items below in the order of greatest personal importance to you (1 being the most important). Discuss your responses in a group to determine the needs of the group.

☐ Personal pride in my job

☐ Awards and honors

☐ Recognition from superiors

☐ Social friendships with coworkers

☐ Personal self-development

☐ Money and tangible rewards

☐ An outlet for complaints

☐ Security for the future

☐ Doing productive work

☐ Pleasant working atmosphere

☐ Open lines of communication

☐ Exciting goals and objectives

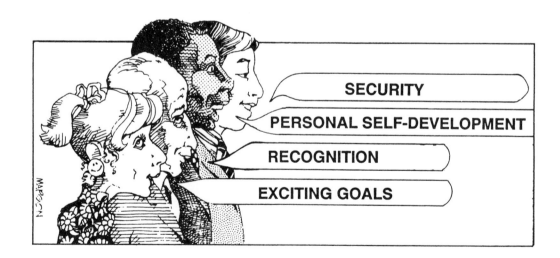

# WHAT CAN WE HOPE TO ACHIEVE?

Optimists can achieve new and profitable opportunities for growth. Pessimists only achieve the traditional gripe sessions that "get it all out on the table" without producing results.

> An *Optimist* sees an opportunity behind every obstacle.
>
> A *Pessimist* sees an obstacle behind every opportunity.

Business books and magazines constantly bombard us with new ways to quick-fix our troubles. There are new theories, new systems, new names and new gurus to fit almost every situation and solve every problem.

Leaders and managers often fear that unless they keep up with all the latest approaches they risk missing the boat. But the celebrated troubles of mega giants in the early 1990s—declining markets, huge layoffs, dramatic changes in the offices and the plants—only point to the fact that security is uncertain and change is inevitable even for the most formidable organizations.

These and other corporate giants invest in all the latest training. They have the resources to buy into every "quality" program, every "customer service" approach and every "teambuilding" movement. But unless these giants—and any other major corporation, small business, sole proprietorship or professional organization—develop internal renewal, the chances of total success from any quick-fix system will never meet the expected objectives.

THE RENEWAL PROCESS: GETTING STARTED

# THE RENEWAL PROCESS: GETTING STARTED

If you've ever seen a well that drew water with a hand pump, you know that to get the flow started you have to pour water down the pipe first. This "priming the pump" creates a vacuum that initiates the flow. Once primed, the water will flow until the suction is broken.

With renewal, you also have to prime the pump. You have to give something by way of commitment to get an abundant return.

## Taking Our Temperature

If a person gets sick, there is usually a fever—the body temperature reacts to the illness. When problems develop in the workplace, the heat is also turned up. Companies must make drastic decisions that affect employees' jobs, careers, plans and dreams.

When a person is ill, the doctor begins the diagnosis by taking the patient's temperature. When a company is affected by change or disruption, taking the temperature is a necessary first step.

Taking the temperature can be as simple as answering a few questions that reveal employees' states-of-mind. The feedback may be shared and discussed and ideas will begin to emerge. It is important to start properly with openness rather than with complaints, criticisms or attempts to give immediate solutions.

# Inspirational Motivation Assessment

*What cause motivates you?*

_____

_____

_____

_____

_____

*What recent inspiration have you experienced?*

_____

_____

_____

_____

_____

*Who would benefit if you renewed your life for the better?*

_____

_____

_____

_____

_____

# THE RENEWAL OF VALUES

Renewal is often a response to an internal sense that the time is ripe for a new level of maturity and we must act now.

What would our world be like if people lived together in harmony on the planet, believed in personal responsibility, and learned from the past so as not to commit the same errors and mistakes. Isn't this what we all seek in our own families and workplace? But motivation is not enough. In recent decades we were on a mad tear toward instant success and wound up with more problems than we could solve, more businesses and buildings than we needed, more government programs than we could support, more environmental damage than we could fix, and more citizens in jail because of greed, self-interest and abuse of other people's rights. The element missing in most of our actions is VALUES.

## Linking Motivation to Values

The "quality" revolution teaches that when motivation is linked to VALUES we actually profit more. In the automobile industry when companies were motivated to build a better vehicle that contained better safety and reliability for the customer they sold more cars and made more profit. This story is the same in every industry, business and organization that linked motivation and VALUES to produce greater results.

Four basic human values have not changed over the entire course of man's existence. The basic values are:

VALUE #1  SECURITY

VALUE #2  RECOGNITION

VALUE #3  SELF-EXPRESSION

VALUE #4  MONEY

## VALUE #1: SECURITY

The order of the basic values needs to be arranged by each individual to suit his or her own present situation. There is a growing gap between what people value and the ability to satisfy those values.

The structure of the workforce and the personal interests of individuals have changed. We have changed from an industrial society to a service society and from a national economy to a global economy. We have changed from a *consumer*-oriented society to a *customer*-oriented society.

> • In the consumer society, the primary emphasis was on the product and service.
>
> • In a customer society, the primary emphasis is on the person who buys or uses the product or service.

We can no longer operate under past assumptions in dealing with people. We either adjust or we lose.

*Security is the primary value sought by most people in the workforce.*

New technology has changed the output-to-employee ratio quickly and drastically. Fewer people can do more with the same or better results. Even though statistics may show that new technology creates jobs, it's difficult to accept this when the job being shifted is yours. Nothing creates more worker motivation than reinforcing a person's employment security. And nothing unmotivates people as much as apprehension about job security.

Of course the value of security is much deeper than just job security. It involves life and health issues, freedom from bodily harm or property loss and financial stability.

# THE RENEWAL OF VALUES (continued)

▶ What areas of security are most important for you? _____

_____

_____

▶ What would you require to feel comfortably secure? _____

_____

_____

▶ How does security affect your workplace? _____

_____

_____

## VALUE #2: RECOGNITION

On a global scale, people all over the world seek recognition as independent nations. Minority groups and individuals spend years, lifetimes, seeking proper recognition. And each of us want to be recognized by others who have some control over our plans and destiny.

▶ What aspects of recognition are of most importance to you? _____

_____

_____

▶ What recognition is lacking? _____

_____

_____

▶ What recognition do you appreciate most? _____

_____

_____

## VALUE #3: SELF-EXPRESSION

Self expression, the desire to be heard and understood, caused language to be created. It is why people write books, compose music, create works of art, write letters to the editor or call in to a radio talk show.

*In 1993, a survey showed that Oprah Winfrey was the highest paid person in the entertainment industry and all she does is serve as a host for people who want to express themselves.*

In the job world, self expression creates workgroups, surveys and discussions. Companies and individuals who allow or even encourage self-expression among colleagues create a better workplace, contribute to problem solving and decrease fear and anxiety.

▶ In what ways has self-expression benefited you in your job or career?

_____

_____

_____

▶ What aspects of self-expression do you consider most important for the benefit of your organization?

_____

_____

_____

▶ What areas need the most improvement?

_____

_____

_____

# THE RENEWAL OF VALUES (continued)

## VALUE #4: MONEY

Money means any tangible exchange medium; there are tribes in parts of the world that use cattle and goats for money. Money is important to us because with it we can attempt to buy the other three values: Security, Recognition, and Self-expression. Money is of little value in and of itself, but can be exchanged for things we seek and desire.

► If you won $1 million dollars in a lottery ($50,000 a year before taxes for twenty years), how would it affect your life?

_____

_____

_____

_____

_____

_____

_____

_____

► If you won $20 million dollars in a lottery ($1 million dollars a year before taxes for 20 years), how would it affect your life?

_____

_____

_____

_____

_____

_____

_____

_____

► If your income suddenly increased ($100.00 a week/$1,000.00 a month), how would you satisfy the primary values:

1. *Security*

_____

_____

_____

_____

2. *Recognition*

_____

_____

_____

_____

3. *Self-expression*

_____

_____

_____

_____

4. *Money*

_____

_____

_____

_____

# HOW IMAGE IMPACTS RENEWAL

Each of us is unique with our own creative talents, personal image and belief structure.

Fred Allen, the great radio comedian, once said,

*"You only go around once in life, but if you work it right, once is enough."*

You are not just the result of your parents' genes. You are also the result of what you have allowed yourself to be. You act like the person you perceive yourself to be. We call this your image.

There are three forms of image that affect us in both our personal lives and our careers.

## 1. SELF-IMAGE
## 2. PROJECTED IMAGE
## 3. PERCEIVED IMAGE

### 1. SELF-IMAGE

This is how you see yourself, your personal self-evaluation. Your self-image can be either positive or negative. Only you determine which it is at any moment. Self-image consists of:

**a.** Your *Biological Image*—your physical self—body image.

**b.** Your *Psychological Image*—you in relationship to your social environment—other people.

**c.** Your *Spiritual Image*—you in relationship to a supreme being, to beauty, truth, honesty, faith, hope, love and all other ideals.

Self-image is probably the single greatest factor in determining happiness, success and fulfillment. There can be no renewal without coming to grips with our own self-image.

# A Self-Image Evaluation

*What do I think of "myself"?*

_____

_____

_____

*What is positive about me?*

_____

_____

_____

*What is negative about me?*

_____

_____

_____

*What personal change would boost my self-image the most?*

_____

_____

_____

# HOW IMAGE IMPACTS RENEWAL (continued)

## 2. PROJECTED IMAGE

This is how we want others to see us. We work hard to project the proper image, spending huge sums of money on cosmetics, jewelry, clothing and cars, etc. But we also unintentionally project an image by the ways we speak and react to others both verbally and with body language.

A company or organization also has a **Projected Image.**

Companies spend money, time and effort to get people to believe they are ''the best,'' ''the most dependable,'' ''the most caring.''

*What image do you want to project personally?*

_____

_____

_____

_____

*What area of your personal image needs to be strengthened?*

_____

_____

_____

_____

*What image does your organization want to project?*

_____

_____

_____

_____

## 3. PERCEIVED IMAGE

This is how other people see us. Our perceived image is controlled by others. People experience us from their perspective not ours. Sometimes we don't know how other people perceive us because they don't reveal their thoughts. But it's difficult to hide actions. People treat us the way they perceive us. In a renewed organization, people are encouraged to be honest without being cruel. Sometimes the only way to understand how other people perceive us is to ask them.

*How do other people perceive me?*

_____

_____

_____

_____

*How do I know?*

_____

_____

_____

_____

If you are willing, have several people in a group write a paragraph about how they perceive you. This can be done with others as a group exercise.

ARE YOU READY FOR RENEWAL?

# AM I READY FOR RENEWAL?

Am I open to the process? To find out place a check by each item that you feel applies to you.

## *Renewal Checklist*

☐ I am aware of reasons why we need change within my workgroup.

☐ I am willing to open myself up to scrutiny.

☐ I feel confident about the judgments I am making.

☐ I am flexible and can adjust to suit the needs of others.

☐ I am free of critical feelings and have an open attitude.

☐ I am willing to make new commitments to create lasting Renewal.

If you answered yes to three or more, you are ready to start the process.

# A Self-Evaluation Checklist

*What do I want?* _____

_____

_____


*Who can help me get it?* _____

_____

_____


*How should I approach them?* _____

_____

_____


*What other options are open to me?* _____

_____

_____


*When can I expect to achieve my objectives?* _____

_____

_____


*What changes do I need to make to accomplish my objectives?* _____

_____

_____

# IS MY WORKPLACE READY FOR RENEWAL?

*The future doesn't just happen, we create it.*

We can't leave the future to chance. Every decision we make affects our future.

The success of a company, department or workgroup, depends on the people involved making fast, accurate assessments of a situation, working out a decision with a sense of urgency and cooperation, and moving on to the next issue.

### That is what RENEWAL is all about!

It is always much easier to deal with mathematical certainties than with the changing human state of affairs. No people in all of human history have had to adjust to more change than the people living in the second half of the twentieth century. The post World War II decades affected the economies of the world in rapid and mystifying ways.

- The 1950s were the era of the cold war with military-industrial buildup providing jobs.

- The 1960s created jobs based on the space race.

- The 1970s created jobs based on the computer high-tech revolution.

- The 1980s created jobs based on the communications revolution.

- The 1990s created jobs based on the synergistic changes taking place in all those industries and revolutions.

When rapid, fundamental change upsets industries, economies, jobs and careers, it is time to renew the workforce. Companies that recognize and address the need for renewal find two major benefits: enhanced performance and improved morale.

# RENEWAL ENHANCES PERFORMANCE

Fewer people are doing more work with fewer resources. Work distribution has become a major factor in maintaining productivity and achieving goals and objectives. Productivity measured strictly by quantity is being upgraded to productivity based on quality. And, in most cases, where cultural appreciation is encouraged the numbers hold their own and even increase.

Statistics indicate that reducing stress increases performance and productivity. Some companies go far beyond adjusting high-anxiety work schedules and deadlines to provide employees with outlets for a changing lifestyle. Some provide day-care centers for children of employees, employee fitness and exercise programs, weight-control programs, or even smoking, drinking, drug and alcohol counseling. These employee assistance programs (EAPs), vary with each provider but all are intended to promote "wellness," which in turn promotes better job performance.

In keeping with the spirit of renewal, companies are offering educational programs and courses not directly related to job training: philosophy, psychology, cultural diversity appreciation, nature and environmental awareness and music appreciation.

*A Rule of Thumb: Taking good care of your employees pays big dividends.*

# ADDRESSING EMPLOYEES' CONCERNS IMPROVES MORALE

When times are changing and belt tightening is necessary, or when major shifts have taken place—employees have more questions than answers:

✓ Are we reviewing and controlling the outflow of expenses and time-consuming tasks and activities?

✓ Are we making the most of the resources available and spreading the work flow to prevent downtime and keep people involved?

✓ Are we opening the lines of communication between internal and external operations?

✓ Are we paying greater attention to current customers and clients?

✓ Are we involving everyone in the workforce more actively in decisions affecting their individual departments or work assignments?

✓ Are we building credibility with customers by offering service and satisfaction above and beyond the call of duty?

✓ Are we developing greater credibility internally by listening to the input from the people who perform the job?

✓ Besides compensation and benefits, are we offering genuine psychological rewards such as recognition and respect that starts at the top and flows throughout the organization?

✓ Are we offering flexible choices so workers at all levels can make responsible decisions that enable them to perform their job and home related duties more effectively?

## Does My Workplace:

► Produce products and services that people need and want.

- They're not intimidated by changing market requirements.
- They go directly to the marketplace to do research.
- They freely accept feedback from within the workforce.

► Strive for quality and make it easy to do business.

- They actually believe the golden rule is more than just lip service.

---

**Do Unto Others As You Would Have Others Do Unto You!**

---

- They prevent poor quality in products and services before it happens.

► Believe that personality affects performance.

- They create an atmosphere of positive, professional, team work.
- They recognize that people require both physical and psychological rewards and they invest in their people as a valuable asset.
- They recognize and expect leadership at every level from top to bottom.

► Manage their resources well

- They know when to spend and when to save.
- They know when to grow and when to maintain stability.
- They know when to diversify and when to centralize, streamline and consolidate.

# *Work Morale and Needs Assessment*

High morale is an attitude of confidence and satisfaction that results from effective job stimulation. When we feel we are accomplishing our objectives and are being adequately rewarded we have high morale. When we are in a state of confusion or have negative attitudes our morale will be low.

1. Rate your present state of morale on a scale of 1 to 10 and respond to the following questions to further define your position.

   *LOW*                                                          *HIGH*
   1     2     3     4     5     6     7     8     9     10

   If high—WHY? _____

   _____

   _____

   If low—WHY? _____

   _____

   _____

2. What are the primary job stresses you have to cope with? _____

   _____

   _____

   _____

   _____

3. What is the best part of your job? _____

   _____

   _____

   _____

   _____

4. What do you like least about your job? _____

_____

_____

_____

_____

5. What training do you think would help you to be more effective? _____

_____

_____

_____

_____

6. What is the most important contribution you feel you make to the organization?

_____

_____

_____

_____

7. What problems need to be solved to ensure better teamwork? _____

_____

_____

_____

_____

8. What questions most concern you regarding your role with the organization?

_____

_____

_____

_____

# ASSESSMENT REVIEW

Survey responses from 4,500 participants indicated the following:

### *REASONS FOR HIGH MORALE, ACCORDING TO PRIORITY:*

#1—Security in job—optimistic about company.
#2—Respect and fairness from superiors.
#3—Team spirit in the work group; able to discuss problems openly.

### *OTHERS*

- Recognition from superiors.
- Freedom to do your job.
- Sense of humor among work group.

### *REASONS FOR LOW MORALE, ACCORDING TO PRIORITY:*

#1—Work overload.
#2—Lack of incentive to do a good job.
#3—Disorganization.

### *OTHERS:*

- Low pay.
- Lack of recognition.
- Lack of communication.

*Comment:* The level of morale always increased after renewal programs, indicating that when managers, supervisors and workers had an opportunity to develop, grow and communicate, they increased their positive attitudes and productivity.

Technical training of itself does not boost morale. Reeducation that helps people adjust to new technology has a significant effect on employee attitude throughout the entire organization.

# SECTION

## II

## Obstacles to Renewal

# STRESS IN THE WORKFORCE

Renewing the workforce alleviates unacceptable levels of stress in some or all areas of the workplace.

Stress is a normal occurrence that we learn to live with. But at times, stress robs us of peace of mind and body. Renewal is a way to reexamine our job stress, to understand it better and apply coping skills to relieve it.

► Take an accounting of your *personal* and *job* related stresses.

► Define the top stresses in each category.

► Trace the origin of each stress by asking ''why'' questions.

► Define an acceptable goal or objective that you control for:
  • Eliminating the stress
  • Coping with it

► Choose a coping technique that will help you deal with the pressure.

Not all stress and pressure is bad. Pressures causes headaches.
Pressure also causes diamonds.

# *Stress Inventory*

| WORK-RELATED STRESS<br>Check any that apply: | PERSONAL STRESS<br>Check any that apply: |
|---|---|
| ☐ Time Pressures and Deadlines | ☐ Lack of Security |
| ☐ Work Overload | ☐ Lack of Self-confidence |
| ☐ Role Conflicts | ☐ Lack of Education |
| ☐ Conflicts with Subordinates | ☐ Lack of Personal Motivation |
| ☐ Conflicts with Superiors | ☐ Lack of Experience |
| ☐ Getting Others to Cooperate | ☐ Lack of Financial Resources |
| ☐ Lack of Sufficient Equipment | ☐ Lack of Goals |
| ☐ Lack of Sufficient Financial Resources | ☐ Lack of an Organized Agenda |
| ☐ Lack of Goals or Guidelines | ☐ Lack of Ability to Deal with Others |
| ☐ Lack of Communication | ☐ Lack of Ability to Deal with Personal Problems |
| ☐ Lack of Decisions | ☐ Lack of Training |
| ☐ Lack of Sufficient Information | ☐ Other |
| ☐ Other | |

Which are the top three that need to be solved?

1. _____

2. _____

3. _____

What risks must you take to solve them?

_____

_____

_____

Which are the top three that need to be solved?

1. _____

2. _____

3. _____

What risks must you take to solve them?

_____

_____

_____

# ROADBLOCKS TO RENEWAL

There are five major pressure points that must be addressed by organizations as they prepare to undergo renewal of the workforce.

## 1. DOUBT

Doubt is a state of uncertainty. There are always reasons to resist change and the first is usually a lack of belief that change can take place. But change can and will take place. In some instances, it must take place or we could lose our jobs, our clients or even our organization. ''You Gotta Believe.''

## 2. FEAR

Fear is a threat. Remove the threat and you remove the fear. The three primary types of fear are:

> Fear of the Unknown
>
> Fear of Rejection
>
> Fear of Failure

One of the best ways to address these fears is to hear how other people succeeded in spite of them.

## 3. ANXIETY

Anxiety is a problem that hasn't happened yet. Anxiety can churn your stomach and make you physically sick, but it isn't real. It's a fear of a future situation that doesn't have to happen.

# ROADBLOCKS TO RENEWAL (continued)

## 4. SPEED

Speed is the inordinate desire for immediate satisfaction in our competitive culture. It is a major contributor to a breakdown in quality and completeness. Speed is often the culprit behind poor decisions and mistakes. Rushing through renewal would be a mistake, because renewal isn't a program, it's a process that requires maturity and an adjustment of our workstyle.

## 5. GREED

Greed is a selfish interest. Greed is an exploitation of the system in a way that ignores the needs of others. Greed is often based on fear and is evident at every level of the workforce. To be successful the renewal process has to focus on personal responsibility. The first step in combating greed is to make people aware that we all need each other to adjust to change.

The primary obstacles to renewal should not end the experience but rather show all the more reason why renewal is needed. Allow the obstacles to surface and deal with them by judging the actions of people rather than the persons themselves.

# JOB BURNOUT

When people burn out on the job, they become depressed, nervous or even physically sick. No one is immune from burnout regardless of their length of time on the job or their level of authority or responsibility. Job burnout is the result of stress caused by a person being required to perform functions over a length of time for which they are not prepared or to which they cannot adjust.

## SYMPTOMS OF BURNOUT

- Insecurity about job or career.
- Inability to adapt to change.
- A feeling of overload with no hope of ever catching up.
- A breakdown of social relationships with coworkers.
- A feeling that no one is listening or cares.

**There are three things that can be done to solve burnout.**

**1.** Change the person.

**2.** Change the job.

**3.** Change the person's attitude about the job.

In some cases you need to do all three.

## 1. Change the person.

- Test the person to see if they have the necessary skills, temperament, and personality to accomplish the job objectives.
- Train or retrain the person with the skills necessary for their job.
- Give the person a temporary assignment, doing another job, to determine if the job roles and responsibilities are the actual reason for the stress.
- Determine if aging or family circumstances have affected the person's ability to continue at a job that may no longer suit their circumstances.

# JOB BURNOUT (continued)

## 2. Change the job.

- Is the job well defined?

- Is stress necessarily a part of the job?

- Can the job be reexamined and changed?

- Are the equipment and tools proper for the job?

> If you assigned a person to cut down a large tree and supplied him with a sledgehammer, one could conclude that the tool needs to be changed. An axe or chain saw would be better suited for the job.

## 3. Change the person's attitude about the job.

- Does the person know why this job is necessary?

- Has the person seen the final product or service that results from the job?

- Is the person being influenced by others in a negative way?

- Does the person need a rest? A vacation?

Dealing with burnout may be beyond the expertise of group members and coworkers. Professional assistance may be advisable. It's much better for the individual and the organization if the situation is faced honestly.

*Some common ways to deal with stress are:*

► Be realistic. Age and different circumstances require periodic adjustment.

► Diet, exercise and relaxation have a definite effect on the body and the mind.

► Low impact exercise, such as a 45-minute walk three times a week, can have a very beneficial effect on attitude as well as the muscles. (Proper medical supervision is advised.)

► Have a heart-to-heart talk with an advisor or friend.

# CONFLICT

*If a person wants to have a place in the sun,*
*that person must learn to live with blisters.*

### 1. Identify the Real Problem.

- Look beneath the symptoms and emotions.

  *Statement:* *"I hate this job."*

  ***Response:*** ***"Why do you feel you hate this job?"***

### 2. Control the Reaction.

- Think before you speak or act.

- Ask questions that require an open response.

  ***Response example:*** ***"Why do you say that?"***

### 3. Avoid Taking All the Responsibility.

- Involve other people.

- Get over the "I" problem.

  *Statements like:* *"I believe—I think—I want"*

  ***Should become:*** ***"What do you believe we should do?"***

  ***"What do you think? What do you want?"***

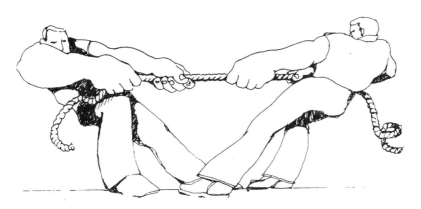

# CONFLICT (continued)

## Allow Conflicts to Surface

- Take your temperature, either as an individual or as an organization.
- Convert conflict language to diplomatic language.
- Give everyone a chance. Do not let a few dominate.
- Get below emotions and feelings by asking clarifying questions rather than always giving answers.
- Do not try to change negative people. Neutralize them.
- Keep the lines of communication open.
- Follow up on complaints. Give assurance that action is being taken.

## Conflict and Self-Assessment

Did it ever occur to you that sometimes when you are in conflict with another person—it may be *your* fault?

## Give Yourself a Reality Check

☐ Do you know what you are talking about?

   — Do you have valid information?

☐ Do you know what the other person is talking about?

   — Most conflicts are based on misunderstandings.

☐ Have you asked clarifying questions?

☐ Do you understand the role of the other party?

   — Is there a role conflict?

☐ Are you open to suggestions, compromise, and change?

☐ Are emotions and feelings getting in the way of a solution?

# CRITICISM

John Dewey, the famed educator said, ''The deepest urge in human nature is the desire to be important.'' If people make mistakes and are criticized, they do not feel important. If people make mistakes and are fairly evaluated, they can retain their self-respect. They tend to correct the mistakes and can be motivated to be more responsible.

## Changing Criticism into Evaluation

### Criticism is a Judgmental Comment.

It is fault finding. It shows disapproval. Criticism indicates like or dislike, good or bad.

### Evaluation is an Indication of Value or Worth.

Evaluation appraises the total situation and seeks a solution. Evaluation is specific and to the point. It lets the person know what is wrong or needs correction without attacking the person. Evaluation reduces guilt and blame. Evaluation requires that we indicate *why* something is not right.

Criticism is easy if it doesn't carry with it the responsibility of finding a solution. If we are held responsible for everything we say or do, either individually or in a group, we soon come to realize that evaluation is a better response than criticism.

---

## AN EFFECTIVE EVALUATION

1. Focuses on the Act, Not the Person.

2. Is Done at the Proper Time and Place.

3. Employs Realistic Judgment.

4. Suggests a Remedy.

5. Develops and Maintains a Good Relationship.

# WHAT ELSE CAN WE CHANGE?

There are three states-of-mind that we can alter in order to adjust to rapid change: attitudes, habits and reactions.

## ATTITUDES

Each one of us controls our own attitudes. Our attitudes control our thoughts and desires. Positive attitudes generate positive ideas and desires. Negative attitudes generate negative ideas and desires. Since desire is the beginning of all achievement, we control our own achievement.

> *"Human beings, by changing the inner attitude of their minds, can change the outer aspect of their lives."*
>
> —William James

## HABITS

You can teach an old dog new tricks only if the old dog wants to learn the new tricks. It's difficult to eliminate habits that took years to form but it can and should be done.

> *"We are approaching the 21st century, we ought not enter it with 20th century skills."*
>
> —Bernard Petrina

From the executive floor to the shop floor, everyone needs to learn new skills and develop different work habits.

## REACTIONS

The age of information is full of surprises. We cannot always choose what will happen, but we can choose how we react.

Reactions cause wars but also cause peace.

Reactions cause employee hostility but also create cooperation.

In the daily newspaper and on television news we see reaction at work, both for good and for bad. The highest levels of government and industry are not immune. Overreaction is a major cause of disruption, anger and hostility in the workplace.

To solve the problem we desperately need to institute renewal in the organization and begin with ourselves. For the moment the best rule to follow is the one we all learned in first grade.

Count to ten before you react.
Give yourself a "time-out" to
think before you act.

# SECTION

## III

# The 7-Step
# Renewal Process

# STEP 1: GET BACK TO BASICS

Getting back to basics means that we reduce each situation to its simplest, most primary elements.

> Every complicated system that works was once a simple system that worked.

The emphasis is on *basics* not back.

On the first day of practice for the Green Bay Packers, Vince Lombardy, the legendary NFL Coach, would stand in front of some of the best football players in the world, hold a ball in front of their faces and say, "Gentlemen this is a football." This is the same Vince Lombardy who said...

*"Practice does not make perfect. Perfect practice makes perfect."*

Accept advice to be sure you're doing the job right. Continue to do it that way until you discover a better way. Stick to the basics.

People who know the basics and practice them are not prone to use slick techniques and flashy projects. Their success is built on consistency.

# PERSONAL PRIORITIES

Renewal involves learning from the experiences of past generations without going through the experience.

People who lived through the depression of the 1930s and the war years of the 1940s were preoccupied with physical survival. Food rationing, loss of all one's life savings, foxholes and air raid sirens imprinted lasting memories on their minds and spirits.

Those who lived through the experience continue to cling to the values and lifestyles that helped them survive hard times. They learned to do without. They were able to put their activities into proper perspective. They learned to *prioritize.*

Today we're faced with another form of survival: surviving the loss of jobs and careers as we know them. Learning from the older generation, we should put our activities in proper perspective.

---

**Renewal means—*PRIORITIZE*. It means do what counts.
Renewal also means learning how and what to do without.**

---

*We can only inspire others if we are inspired ourselves.
This can only happen if we get our priorities straight
and are committed to achieving results.*

What are your top three priorities for this week? This month?

| This Week | This Month |
|---|---|
| 1. _____<br>_____ | 1. _____<br>_____ |
| 2. _____<br>_____ | 2. _____<br>_____ |
| 3. _____<br>_____ | 3. _____<br>_____ |

# A RENEWAL OF BASIC INTENT

Answer the questions below based on your current knowledge. Compare your responses with others. Determine if there is a need to clarify information in order to achieve consensus.

Why does our organization *Exist?* _____

_____

_____

What is our basic *Purpose?* _____

_____

_____

What is our *Mission?* _____

_____

_____

*Who* do we serve? _____

_____

_____

What are our *Major Contributions* to:

• Our Customers? _____

_____

• Society? _____

_____

• Each Other? _____

_____

# ASSESS BASIC MOTIVATION

Why do we do things?

### WE DO THINGS FOR THREE BASIC REASONS.

1. To gain a **BENEFIT**
2. To prevent a **LOSS**
3. To satisfy a **PASSION** or an **URGE**

## 1. The benefit level determines the motivational level.

If there is a great deal of benefit, we will be highly motivated. If there is little or no benefit, either real or perceived, we will not be motivated.

*A supervisor who is given visible recognition by the boss for quality work in his or her department will encourage subordinates to higher performance.*

## 2. Since we are security seekers, we do not want to lose the things we possess.

Prevention of loss can be a motivator and can lead us to act.

*When flood waters threaten people's lives and property, everyone is motivated to head for the river bank to lay sandbags.*

## 3. Since we are beings who enjoy comfort, satisfying our passions can be a motivator.

Satisfying a passion or urge makes us feel good. We can't alway explain it, we just do it. We enjoy sex, food, cars and hobbies because of that motivational fact.

*People climb mountains, explore caves or start companies for the same reason.*

# The Motivation of Achievement

To achieve satisfaction in the three areas of your life, list the achievements you wish to accomplish in these areas.

▶ *Personal Lifestyle*

Physical *(appearance/activities/relaxation)* _____

_____

Mental *(interests/education/training)* _____

_____

Spiritual *(values/practice)* _____

_____

▶ *Job and Career*

Career path *(job/business)* _____

_____

Financial opportunities *(savings/investments)* _____

_____

Financial responsibilities *(income/expenses)* _____

_____

▶ *Social Relations*

Companion, spouse, children, relatives _____

_____

Coworkers _____

_____

Friends _____

_____

# STEP 2: UNDERSTAND PERSONALITY AND PRODUCTIVITY

The Declaration of Independence states that *"all men are created equal."* It does not say that all men (or women) are created the same.

It takes all kinds of individuals to comprise a successful workplace. If we were all extroverts, who would there be to listen to all our chatter? If we were all introverts, who would stir up the waters to get things moving?

### TYPES OF INDIVIDUALS

- **DEPENDENT**
- **RESPONSIBLE**
- **INDEPENDENT**

## DEPENDENT TYPES

These are people who rely on other people and forces for decisions, aid and assistance. They are not handicapped; they are conditioned to believe they are limited and powerless. They are insecure and consider themselves victims. They may have experienced numerous setbacks and have given up "fighting city hall." They may have a poor self-image, low self-esteem and a lack of self-confidence.

Dependent people are stuck within themselves. They always talk about themselves because that's all they think about. Since dependent people rely heavily on others, they avoid specific responsibilities and are quick to defend themselves to avoid blame.

**The primary problem with dependent people is not laziness but *fear*.**

Willing to work to get the job done, as long as someone else makes the decisions and directs them, they are afraid to make mistakes or fail. It can be difficult to work with dependent individuals. Other workers avoid them or treat them with contempt, disrupting the workplace and the renewal process.

Dependent people need affirmation. Find out what they do right and help them see their success, rather than worry about failures. Affirmation is creative, focused support.

## RESPONSIBLE TYPES

Responsible people have the capacity to produce large quantities of work and are self-starters. They do not require close supervision. Responsible people are capable of fulfilling job assignments and commitments. They prefer to be busy and are usually organized for the sake of efficiency. They believe they have a right to share in the decisions that affect their lives and are willing to accept the discipline necessary to accomplish their assignments. Just as dependent people are conditioned to hold back, responsible people are conditioned to get the job done.

**Responsible people need to be kept informed.**

Responsible people see their job as a contract. They rely on fairness within the scope of that job contract, but sometimes see only their side of the agreement. They often resent dependent people because they think dependent people receive the same benefits without putting forth the same effort. Responsible people are generally not afraid to speak up when they encounter unfairness. There are many different types of personalities within this general category and almost all of them want to be kept informed of what's going on. They intensely dislike hidden agendas and special treatment for a chosen few.

# STEP 2: UNDERSTAND PERSONALITY AND PRODUCTIVITY (continued)

## INDEPENDENT TYPES

Independents are people who think for themselves, prefer to work free of restraints, and have creative talents.

Independent people are "risk takers." They can be intuitive types who have a vivid imagination and a great deal of hope for the future or practical, profit-oriented people who understand the secrets of successful enterprise.

Independent people rely on their own abilities. Fear does not hold them back. They are uncomfortable with outside control forces that hinder them from full expression of their ideas.

**The main problem for independent people is getting agreement and sufficient resources to achieve what they believe are worthwhile goals.**

Independent people feel that responsible people don't take enough risks and do not have a sufficient sense of urgency. They can be impatient with dependent people or can actually work well with them because they need somebody to finish what they start. Independents can be difficult to work with when they insist on their own agenda and way of doing things.

The different personality types can be brought into the renewal process if a resourceful leader understands the strong points and vulnerabilities of each and uses the approach we suggest.

# USING CONDITIONING TO IMPROVE PRODUCTIVITY

Conditioning is a form of educational motivation. Sometimes it is good:

- Firefighters are conditioned to react to the alarm with actions that could save lives.
- Driving a car—We stop at a red light without thinking about the brake and accelerator.
- Using a keyboard—We type information without thinking about each key.

Sometimes it is bad:

- If you're watching TV and see a food commercial, it sends you to the refrigerator.
- If someone objects to a pet idea, it causes you to overreact or get quiet.
- If you break something, it causes anger or even cursing.

While all of us are conditioned to a certain extent, we do have a free will. Many routine things we do are a conditioned response done after repeated actions. A person who is proud of his or her work area will pick up a piece of litter without even thinking about it. This person is conditioned to care.

Renewal involves aspects of both motivation (inspiration) and education. We refer to it as educational motivation because it is systematic rather than emotional. A workforce that has had its motivation addressed in a systematic process has a higher degree of productivity.

*Examples of conditioning:*

- ► Think of yourself slicing a lemon. Now, imagine putting it in your mouth and biting it. Did you salivate and feel an actual reaction to the thought?

- ► Spell the word ''FOLK'' out loud. Now, answer quickly—What is the white of an egg called?

Turn the page up-side down.

> Did you say yolk? Think again! The yolk is the yellow part of an egg. You experienced a conditioned reponse. The white part of an egg, by the way, is the albumen.

# USING CONDITIONING TO IMPROVE PRODUCTIVITY (continued)

*What examples of conditioning can you list?* _____

_____

_____

_____

*When is conditioning not in the best interests of the person?* _____

_____

_____

*The organization?* _____

_____

_____

*What are some examples of ways you may be conditioned?* _____

_____

_____

_____

*What kinds of conditioning do you observe at work, among coworkers?* _____

_____

_____

_____

*What suggestions can you offer to condition members of the work team to develop positive activities?* _____

_____

_____

_____

# STEP 3: ESTABLISH WORK TEAMS

Most people are uneasy with close supervision and control. Unless the person is properly trained and the job is a challenge, lack of control can lead to lack of accountability.

Empowerment and self-managed work teams have risen based on the principle that people who control what they are doing have greater enthusiasm and commitment for the job. And this has proven to be correct.

Empowerment implies that people are respected enough to make decisions at their own level of competence. This implies that people are interested more in cooperation than conflict when the result of the enterprise is beneficial to them individually.

Straight talk with employees is critical. Credibility depends on honesty even if the news is bad. Secret agendas are not acceptable.

According to a survey of more than 4500 supervisors and managers, the qualities they appreciated most in a superior are:

**Fairness (respect)**

**Openness (honesty)**

**Competence**

**Support**

**Decisiveness**

Employees respond best when they are treated like responsible adults even though some don't always act that way.

# *Exercise: Identify Appreciated Qualities*

For your work team, list the **qualities** you **appreciate most** in each category. Discuss your responses with group members.

*Qualities I appreciate most in a SUPERIOR:*

_____

_____

_____

_____

_____

_____

*Qualities I appreciate most in a COWORKER:*

_____

_____

_____

_____

_____

_____

*Qualities I appreciate most in a SUBORDINATE:*

_____

_____

_____

_____

_____

_____

# TEAM BUILDING

## HELP OTHERS SUCCEED

Help people to stop devoting an inordinate amount of time and energy coping with obstacles and barriers. Every contribution we make to a group comes back in unexpected ways. The team builder helps the team get started through small successes that build to greater achievements. When the *individual's* goals conform with the *organization's* goals, the individual will work for and with the organization. When this is not the case, the individual will lack motivation. Inspire people to live up to their potential and be quick to forget weaknesses.

## SEEK OUT POSITIVE PEOPLE

A successful team builder needs a good self image and helps others experience the same feeling. For an individual to be motivated, the individual must first develop positive self attitudes, and be involved with positive people. The team needs to understand that believing is seeing. A primary objective is to allow input from many individuals. People support what they help to create. Make activities enjoyable and beneficial to all participants.

## TAKE RESPONSIBILITY FOR YOUR OWN ACTIONS

A successful team builder realizes that success builds on success. Our limitations are usually self-imposed. The individual who copes with success and setbacks is usually able to excel beyond expectations. Risk is an essential part of all great endeavors, don't allow the blame game to influence decisions. A job needs to be done. Get organized and get on with it.

AN EFFECTIVE TEAM BUILDER WILL:

Establish order, leadership, and format.

Encourage participation of people with different roles.

Consider the human factor as well as factors beyond your control.

Operate with the attitude that mutual benefits are more important than mutual satisfaction. (*Everyone may have to let go of the past.*)

Follow through on suggestions and decisions. Deliver what is promised.

# STEP 4: DEFINE TEAM MEMBERS' ROLES

In successful organizations, every person on the team needs a clear picture of how his or her role fits into the total scheme of the enterprise.

▶ A *Role Description* defines expected behavior (who we are.)

▶ A *Job Description* is specific and focused on job activity (what we do.)

A role description shows each person how his or her job interrelates with other departments, other people, other jobs, and other roles. It is always beneficial to know how each person relates to the finished product or service and how the final product or service is sold or used.

Every year at football season, the number one question on many minds is, "Who will be the starting quarterback?" This is a role question.

Our role defines our place in the structure of the organization. The role should tell us and others our level of authority and responsibility.

When roles are confused...

- Decisions are delayed because no one feels a specific responsibility to make the decision.

- Competitors want someone else to take the blame for a potential failure.

- Different people make conflicting demands on the same individual because they have a distorted image of the person's role.

- People "pass the buck."

- Manipulation and job "politics" become excessive.

ROLE PROBLEM RESOLUTION

# Problem Resolution

Role problems can be resolved by:

- Clearly defining each person's role and communicating it to all involved.

- Providing the resources necessary to carry out the role.

- Requiring accountability.

- Being realistic about the number of responsibilities and the time for completing each job.

| A Sample<br>ROLE DESCRIPTION | A Sample<br>JOB DESCRIPTION |
|---|---|
| *Name:* Taylor Lee<br><br>*Title:* Administrative Manager<br><br>*Accountability:* General Manager<br><br>*Role:*<br><br>The Administrative Manager is the person responsible for maintaining effective office operations and complete records of all transactions. | *Name:* Taylor Lee<br><br>*Title:* Administrative Manager<br><br>*Accountability:* General Manager<br><br>*Job Description:*<br><br>• Interview and hire all new personnel<br><br>• Maintain training programs<br><br>• Assign office assistants in all areas of operations<br><br>• Investigate and purchase all office equipment<br><br>• Conduct staff meetings on a weekly basis<br><br>• Complete weekly reports to General Manager |
| **A Role Description is General.** | **A Job Description is Specific.** |

## Role Description Form

NAME _____

TITLE _____

ACCOUNTABILITY _____

ROLE _____

_____

_____

_____

EXPECTATIONS _____

_____

_____

_____

_____

| PRIMARY RESPONSIBILITIES | ACCOUNTABLE TO |
|---|---|
|  |  |

# STEP 5: ENCOURAGE COMMUNICATION

We live in the Information Age. In spite of all the marvels we have already seen, we are only at the dawn of a great communications era. Everthing from primitive sign language, to the invention of the printing press, through the age of radio and television will be surpassed in new, breathtaking, instantaneous communications using satellites and wireless technology. But we still have problems getting the information we need to accomplish our tasks.

Communications renewal requires attention to the human factor because the human factor is the primary cause of error, miscommunication and misinterpretation.

> Communication is the ability to convey meaning
> from one mind to another.

Individuals who control communications control events and ideas.

### *The purpose of communication is to* inform *and to* influence.

Renewal requires that we strive for both objectives in all our communications. Solving only one will not help us to communicate with desired effectiveness. If we inform but fail to influence, people know what to do but don't do it. And if we influence but fail to properly inform, people make decisions based on ignorance and misinformation.

# BARRIERS TO EFFECTIVE COMMUNICATION

To build bridges instead of fences, we have to identify and remove existing barriers.

Place a checkmark by any barriers to effective communication that you encounter.

_____ ORAL RATHER THAN WRITTEN TRANSMISSION

_____ LACK OF EVALUATION OR FEEDBACK

_____ TOO MANY PERSONS INVOLVED

_____ INSUFFICIENT INFORMATION

_____ LACK OF UNDERSTANDING

_____ RULES AND REGULATIONS

_____ MISTAKES AND ERRORS

_____ POOR TRANSMISSION

_____ PROCRASTINATION

_____ ULTERIOR MOTIVES

_____ DISORGANIZATION

_____ LACK OF DECISION

_____ HASTY RESPONSE

_____ OVERLOAD

_____ POLITICS

_____ OTHER

Combine your results with others. Determine the top five barriers by adding the items with the most 1's and 2's, etc.

# Successful Communication Requirements

Successful Renewal requires that all persons:

✓ *Actively* communicate with each other.

✓ Are *willing* to listen and receive feedback.

✓ Are *united* with common *goals* and *purpose*.

Every communication whether written or verbal has five important elements. To improve communications, we need to understand each of the elements and see how each contributes to developing more effective communications.

## *The Elements of Communication*

1. The Sender—*The sender is the transmitter.*

2. The Receiver—*The receiver is the interpreter.*

3. The Message—*The message is the content.*

4. The Method—*The method is the medium.*

5. The Effect—*The effect is the result.*

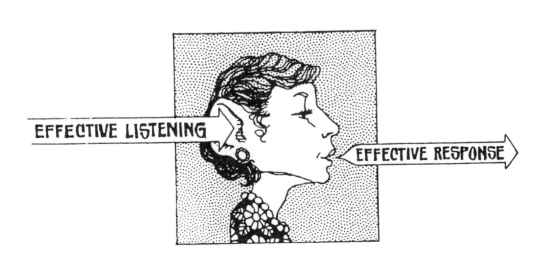

# *Exercise: Effective Communications*

1. What characteristics do you expect of the **sender** of an effective communication?

   _____

   _____

   _____

2. What characteristics are needed by the **receiver**?

   _____

   _____

   _____

3. What are the characteristics of a **message** that cause you to notice it?

   _____

   _____

   _____

4. How do you determine the best **method** for delivering a communication?

   _____

   _____

   _____

5. What can the sender do to ensure that the receiver will achieve the proper **effect**?

   _____

   _____

   _____

How would you apply the five elements of an effective communication to these examples so that you get a satisfactory result?

1. The president of your company issues a request that all employees submit a list of office equipment needs by the end of the current month.

_____

_____

_____

_____

_____

_____

2. You discovered a possible mistake on a printed piece that has already gone to the printer.

_____

_____

_____

_____

_____

_____

3. A speaker you scheduled for an important meeting tomorrow morning is ill and can't be there for the presentation and you have to get a substitute.

_____

_____

_____

_____

_____

_____

# USE DIPLOMATIC LANGUAGE

To increase cooperation and reduce conflict, use diplomatic language rather than conflict language.

| CONFLICT LANGUAGE | DIPLOMATIC SUBSTITUTE |
|---|---|
| Do this... | Here's what needs to be done. |
| You're wrong... | Why do you say that? |
| I disagree... | Here's how I see it. |
| You are confusing me... | This is confusing to me. |
| You made a mistake... | This is not right. |
| I can't... | Let's see what we can do? |
| It's not my job... | We'd better check with... |
| What's the problem?... | Tell me what happened. |
| Who did it?... | What happened? |

EVERY COMMUNICATION IS AT THE
MERCY OF ITS ENVIRONMENT

# *Exercise: Practice Language Substitution*

List examples of conflict language you hear on the job and suggest a diplomatic substitute.

| CONFLICT LANGUAGE | DIPLOMATIC SUBSTITUTE |
|---|---|
| 1. _____ | 1. _____ |
| 2. _____ | 2. _____ |
| 3. _____ | 3. _____ |
| 4. _____ | 4. _____ |
| 5. _____ | 5. _____ |
| 6. _____ | 6. _____ |
| 7. _____ | 7. _____ |
| 8. _____ | 8. _____ |
| 9. _____ | 9. _____ |

# COMMUNICATING AT MEETINGS

Meetings are the most common vehicle for interaction and problem solving. A meeting should never waste time. Meetings need to be properly planned and have a positive purpose.

## A *GOOD* MEETING:

- Has a clearly defined purpose and goals
- Is audience oriented
- Opens lines of communication
- Promotes self-expression and willing participation
- Appeals to the senses and comfort
- Encourages involvement in planning
- Leader keeps the meeting under control
- Motivates participants to change
- Ends with a specific "Call to Action"
- Starts and ends on time

## A *POOR* MEETING:

- Lacks preparation
- Lacks a defined purpose
- Begins with an apology
- Is rushed
- Has a hit-and-miss structure
- Is sandwiched between other activities
- Lacks time limits
- Repeats routine matters
- Lacks assertive leadership
- Has dictatorial leadership
- Has an uncomfortable atmosphere
- Doesn't solve problems
- Lacks free and open expression
- Lacks participation
- Is concerned with "getting out of here"

# A Meeting Leader's Checklist

Check yourself to be sure all areas are covered.

☐ Pre-meeting preparation.

☐ Assign roles and responsibilities.

☐ Define goals and objectives.

☐ Set up the agenda and schedule.

☐ Make sure all logistics are handled.

☐ Notify people to attend.

☐ Define exercises for participation.

☐ Prepare handout materials.

☐ Prepare visuals.

☐ Set time limits.

☐ Prepare responses to settle potential conflicts and disagreements.

☐ Prepare speakers.

☐ Define room set-up.

☐ Keep a record of information.

☐ Provide refreshment breaks.

☐ Define a call to action and follow-up procedures.

# COMMUNICATING AT MEETINGS
## (continued)

## General Rules to Renew Communications

**1.** *Clarify the message* you intend to communicate.

**2.** *Communicate with the proper intent* avoiding conflict language.

**3.** Be sure the *communication is transmitted and received properly.*

**4.** *Encourage* and *provide feedback.*

## General Rules to Renew Listening

**1.** Focus on meanings. Clarify if necessary.

**2.** Withhold judgment.

**3.** Don't interrupt.

**4.** Respond properly.

# STEP 6: ESTABLISH EXPECTATIONS

Renewal is not a return to the way things were.

> "You can't go home again."
> "You never step into the same river twice."

Or as Earl Wilson wrote:

> *"When you return to the town of your youth, you realize it isn't the town you longed for, it is your youth."*

Expectations are often idealistic hopes and dreams that go unfulfilled. Some people have defined and written down their goals. But that is not the norm.

There are, however, several expectations that are universally sought in the workplace. Though these expectations are usually minimum requirements, if they go unmet it becomes a major cause for contention.

## Renewal Must Address These Expectations:

1. *People expect to be treated fairly.*

   ► People want respect as individuals—Equality.

   ► People want respect for individual contributions—Equity.

2. *People expect to be informed.*

   ► Honesty—Tell it like it is.

   ► Understanding—Provide an outlet for feedback.

3. *People expect leaders and managers to be competent and knowledgable.*

   ► Competent
      • Qualified
      • Prepared
      • Proficient

   ► Knowledgeable
      • Aware
      • Reasonable
      • Responsible

# STEP 6 (continued)

**4.** *People expect the support necessary to accomplish the result.*

► Resources

- Financial Resources—Budget
- Human Resources—Sufficient Personnel
- Environmental Resources—Pleasant Workplace

► Tools

- Up-to-date Training
- Proper Equipment that Works
- Good Internal Communications Network

► Advocacy

- Legal Rights Protected
- Sufficient Benefits
- Realistic Policies and Procedures

YOU'VE GOT IT!

# *Quiz: Are Your Expectations Being Met?*

How are expectations being met in your workplace? Evaluate each area of expectation. If the expectation is being met, place a checkmark in the box. If it isn't being met, leave it blank.

## PERSONAL EXPECTATIONS

☐ Treated with Fairness

☐ Equality

☐ Equity

## MANAGEMENT EXPECTATIONS

☐ Competent Management

☐ Knowledgeable Leadership

☐ Qualified Management

☐ Prepared for Achieving Success

☐ Proficient Leadership

☐ Aware Management

☐ Reasonable Management

☐ Responsible Management

## INVOLVEMENT EXPECTATIONS

☐ Kept Informed

☐ Honesty

☐ Outlets for Feedback

## POLICY AND PROCEDURE EXPECTATIONS

☐ Sufficient Financial Resources

☐ Sufficient Personnel

☐ Pleasant Workplace

☐ Up-to-Date Training

☐ Proper Equipment that Works

☐ Good Internal Communications

☐ Legal Rights Protected

☐ Sufficient Benefits

☐ Realistic Policies and Procedures

If you have more than six boxes checked or if you have checked several in one category, review the areas you feel don't meet your expectations with your supervisor.

# STEP 7: SET GOALS FOR PRODUCTIVE CHANGE

It is important to set goals. It is even more important to set up the system to carry out the goals. All goals demand productive change. The goalsetter wants to accomplish an objective that is not now being accomplished or that needs to be improved.

The primary "Elements of Productive Change" are listed below. Each goal should be evaluated against these elements. The goal should be written so that the element can be easily followed.

Goals that do not allow the participants to fulfill these elements probably will not be achieved. They should be reviewed—rewritten if necessary, or changed.

### ELEMENT:

1. Jobs should be defined so as to allow the individual to make changes within the scope of his/her responsibility.

   *Write a suggested goal that would reflect productive change.*

   _____

   _____

### ELEMENT:

2. Management needs to recognize and act upon the individual's need for information, direction and approval.

   *Write a suggested goal that would reflect productive change.*

   _____

   _____

### ELEMENT:

3. Management should clarify roles and provide measurable accountability.

   *Write a suggested goal that would reflect productive change.*

   _____

   _____

A *Goal* **is a long-range target** that has a defined plan of action and a specific completion point.

An *Objective* **is a short-range achievement** that helps fulfill the long-range goal.

**Sample Goal:**

> To become proficient in the use of XYZ software on my personal computer, in thirty days.

**Sample Objectives:**

- To read the XYZ manual

- To devote one hour a day to practice

- To complete a sample project each week, using the XYZ program

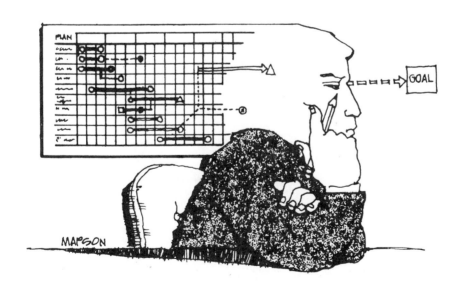

# LIFE AREA GOALS

There are five basic areas of life that are important areas in which to set goals.

| LIFE AREA | SAMPLE GOAL |
|---|---|
| **1.** PERSONAL | *I will lose ten pounds in sixty days.* |
| | _____ |
| | _____ |
| **2.** FAMILY | *I will complete our family vacation plans in six months.* |
| | _____ |
| | _____ |
| **3.** CAREER | *I will become certified with a professional designation in one year.* |
| | _____ |
| | _____ |
| **4.** FINANCIAL | *I will save an extra $200 a month for our upcoming family vacation.* |
| | _____ |
| | _____ |
| **5.** SOCIAL | *I will plan a 4th of July party for my coworkers.* |
| | _____ |
| | _____ |

Renewal requires an atmosphere of shared responsibility; working together in groups or teams to solve problems and develop personal and organizational maturity in the midst of change.

Renewal creates synergy so that we can make orderly and responsible changes.

*Synergy: the action of two or more organisms to achieve an effect of which each is individually incapable.*

# THE TEST OF A CREATIVE GOAL

✓ Is it your own goal?

- If the goal was imposed, it is actually somebody else's goal.

✓ Is the goal written and positive?

- If it is written, it becomes a commitment.
- If it is positive, it encourages success.

✓ Is the goal specific and challenging?

- You can't set a goal to become "better." It must be a specific challenge. Instead of—"I will improve my exercise program," it should be—"I will exercise three times a week."

✓ Is the goal controllable and attainable?

- You can't control a goal "to be the best," but you can control selling 30% more per month which will make you the best.

✓ Is the goal measurable?

- The goal must be able to be broken down into objectives that are measurable. You can't set a goal to be a well-read person. You can set a goal to read two books a week for a year which will make you a well-read person.

# *Goal Plan Form*

Area of life _____

Goal _____

_____

_____

Completion Date _____

Short-term
Objectives

1. _____

_____

2. _____

_____

3. _____

_____

4. _____

_____

Indicate how the goal passes the test of a creative goal.

*Personal* _____

*Written & Positive* _____

*Specific & Challenging* _____

*Controllable and Attainable* _____

*Measurable* _____

# SECTION

# IV

# Strategies for Renewal

# HOW LEADERS CAN MAKE A DIFFERENCE

The process of renewal starts with managers and supervisors and their ability to influence change. There are several techniques that successful supervisors can use to begin the process of workforce renewal. It is necessary to use each of the techniques to achieve the best results. Success can be measured by observing the attitudes and productivity levels of the workers, and supervisors will have the satisfaction of knowing that they are enhancing their management skills as well.

## #1: USE AFFIRMATION

One of the most positive means of support is to affirm one's workforce. Affirmation is a powerful tool in the process of renewal.

Affirmation is linked to support and support is linked to performance, and plays an important role in achieving dreams and goals. Positive support is cited by most researchers as the primary reason for high morale and the lack of positive support as the major cause for low morale.

Find out what people do right and help them see their successes rather than worry about their failures. Affirmation is focused, creative support.

## Leadership Affirmations

I will:

- Make people feel important
- Empower people to make decisions
- Speak to people by name
- Give credit when credit is due
- Listen attentively
- Isolate attention
- Offer praise often

# HOW LEADERS CAN MAKE A DIFFERENCE (continued)

How can you affirm actions of your closest coworkers? _____

_____

_____

In order for renewal to take place, what affirmations are needed within the organization? _____

_____

_____

## #2: BUILD TRUST

A job is not just a contract, it's also a relationship. Trust creates and holds the relationships together.

**When dealing with people, an influencing characteristic that will help create renewal is trust.**

People are often overlooked or taken for granted on a day-to-day basis because they quietly do their job. But people often see their job as a relationship and they expect others to trust and be honest with them.

When trust breaks down between superiors and subordinates or coworkers, it can only be renewed by bringing the parties back into the information loop. People want to know what is going on. Suspicion must be replaced by communication.

If information is ignored or deliberately blocked, the flow of information stops and there is a communication problem. There is no chance of influencing the parties to change if they don't trust each other and this could create conflict. The focus moves from the problem to emotions and feelings. Get back to the core problem by correcting the suspicion.

## #3: PROMOTE PRIDE

We experience pride when persons, possessions or achievements create a high sense of internal assent. Pride generates self-esteem and feelings of gratification.

Pride is a powerful force that can be put to work as an influencing factor to develop renewal.

People can be proud of their

- Accomplishments
- Ideas
- Independence
- Results
- Organization
- Titles
- Recognition by fellow workers

Awards and honors can increase pride which, if properly used, can result in a high degree of productivity, quality and morale.

Influence people by recognizing their efforts and taking advantage of their sense of pride.

# HOW LEADERS CAN MAKE A DIFFERENCE
## (continued)

### #4: SOLVE PROBLEMS

1. *Solve Problems Not Symptoms*

   - List all the symptoms.

   - Make sure everyone agrees on the problem to be solved.

   - Use brainstorming techniques to reach agreement.

2. *Make a List of Options*

   - Don't try to come to a solution until you have considered all the options.

   - Narrow the primary options to three or four that best suit the circumstances.

3. *Make a Decision*

   - Choose one of the suggested options as your decision.

   - Never make a decision based on an option that was not considered.

4. *Take Action*

   - Design specific steps that need to be taken to carry out the decision.

   - Assign responsibility and evaluate as you proceed.

### #5: RESOLVE CONFLICT

There is no such thing as a risk-free environment. Everywhere you turn, there are hazards, obstacles and differences of opinion. Renewed people concentrate on opportunities not obstacles.

Resolving conflict provides us with a vehicle for growth and greater happiness, both on the job and at home. There are several conflict resolution tactics you can use—overcoming stress, criticism and evaluation and communications.

Determine how resolving conflict can benefit you, the parties involved, and the organization. Follow-up with the proper techniques.

1. Neutralize negative people by letting them speak and express themselves.

    — Instead of giving answers, ask questions.

2. Get the parties involved to consider options and possibilities.

3. Finally, get the parties to do one thing at a time with Synergy.

Resolving conflict helps people to open their minds to other points of view.

There is no more capable vehicle to achieve renewal than conflict resolution.

## #6: IMPROVE ATTITUDES

1. *Define what you want to achieve.*

    — Offer illustrations as an example of the ideal outcome.

    — Create a target to shoot for and put a date on it.

2. *Neutralize the negative.*

    — Guide negative to neutral.

    — Then persuade neutral to move to the positive.

    — Gradual change is better than instant conversion.

3. *Use test results and pilot programs to develop positive support.*

    — Try the ideas in small batches before you commit to total accpetance.

    — Ask for feedback as you proceed.

# HOW LEADERS CAN MAKE A DIFFERENCE (continued)

**4.** *Keep people informed.*

- — Communicate the total picture rather than bits and pieces.
- — Give participants a vision of the finished project.

**5.** *Keep the faith.*

- — Don't allow a few negatives to destroy the total effort.
- — Reinforce weak attitudes.
- — Support positive attitudes.
- — Keep everything in its proper perspective.

## #7: PROMOTE OWNERSHIP

*The only way to get from a wish to a goal is to choose the proper vehicle to get you there.*

Strategies are vehicles that help us accomplish our desires. Tactics are the logistics needed to get the vehicles to their destinations.

In a free market society, ownership is a vehicle that creates a sense of security. Owning property and possessions is the most common personal exercise of ownership. Owning your own business or stock are the most common forms of business ownership. Ownership is a perfect strategy to encourage renewal.

### Example of Personal Ownership

- Investing in real estate, mutual funds, collectibles

### Examples of Employee Ownership

- Employee Stock Option Plan
- Employee Owned Companies
- Getting your own office
- Getting your own equipment
- Getting your own company car

# *Examples of Ownership*

Think of all the ways *ownership* could help motivate you and your coworkers to renew your commitments and priorities.

| Personal Ownership | Organizational Ownership |
| --- | --- |
| 1. _____ | 1. _____ |
| 2. _____ | 2. _____ |
| 3. _____ | 3. _____ |
| 4. _____ | 4. _____ |
| 5. _____ | 5. _____ |
| 6. _____ | 6. _____ |
| 7. _____ | 7. _____ |
| 8. _____ | 8. _____ |
| 9. _____ | 9. _____ |
| 10. _____ | 10. _____ |

# HOW LEADERS CAN MAKE A DIFFERENCE (continued)

## #8: ENCOURAGE CONTINUING EDUCATION

Another great strategy for renewal is education. The 21st Century will be a century of phenomenal advances in technology. Now is the time to find our personal niche in the future.

For example, begin by reading about the marvelous technological advances in an area that excites you. Write to companies that engage in that particular field and ask for information and literature. Attend trade shows to see and experience the new technology firsthand. Make educational and career decisions based on what you see and hear. If you "get hooked," you'll never be the same. Your priorities will change to fit your new desires.

*What is the vehicle you wish to pursue?* _____

_____

_____

_____

_____

_____

_____

*What education is necessary to achieve the objectives?* _____

_____

_____

_____

_____

_____

_____

# RENEWAL: POINTS TO REMEMBER

In order for Renewal to succeed or even take place, an attitude of openness is essential.

► People are interested in themselves first. You've got to impress them of the mutual benefits of renewal.

► Everybody thinks their ideas are worthwhile. Don't be too fast in dismissing an idea. Probe and clarify the idea first.

► The reason people argue or disagree is because both sides think they are correct. People fight because they don't know how to argue. Be able to backup your arguments with facts.

► 80% of our decisions are made from emotion, 20% are made from logic. People are influenced by emotional benefits they will receive.

► You can't set goals for others. But you can inspire them to set their own goals. People perform better when they are pursuing goals they set for themselves.

► Everybody is an unfinished product. People can and do change. You may have a sleeping giant in your organization who just needs a wake-up call.

► Challenge is usually met with resistance. You can't change negative people but you can neutralize them. You can change neutral to positive if you do it right.

► Leadership is necessary at all levels. Renewal does not work well in a dictatorial organization.

► Listen! Listen! Listen!

### WORKFORCE RENEWAL

*Depending on our perspective, this is either the worst of times or the best of times. The difference is not in the times, but in our minds.*

*Renewal is a commitment to make this the best of times. If we want to be in touch with the future, we can only do it by getting in touch with ourselves and in touch with the people around us.*

*The future doesn't just happen. We are creating it right now.*

*Begin by doing what is necessary; then do what is possible; soon you will find yourself doing the impossible.*

# REFERENCES

Dichter, Ernest. *The Strategy of Desire.* Garden City, New York: Doubleday and Co., Inc., 1960.

Drucker, Peter F. *Management: Tasks, Responsibilities, Practices.* New York: Harper & Row, 1973.

Gardner, J. W. *Self-Renewal: The Individual and the Innovative Society.* New York: Harper & Row, 1964.

Gilmer, B. VonHaller. Carnegie Mellon University, *Psychology.* New York: Harper & Row, 1973.

Herzberg, Frederick. *Work and the Nature of Man.* Cleveland: World, 1966.

Maslow, Abraham. *Motivation and Personality.* New York: Harper & Row, 1954.

McGregor, Douglas. *The Human Side of Enterprise.* New York: McGraw-Hill, 1960.

Norfolk, Donald. *The Stress Factor.* New York: Simon and Shuster, 1977.

Petrina, Bernard. *Motivating People To Care.* Harrisburg, PA: Renewal Resources, 1989.

Ruch, Floyd L. University of Southern California, *Psychology and Life.* Glenview, IL: Scott Foresman and Co., 1967.

Toffler, Alvin. *Future Shock.* New York: Random House, 1970.

U.S. Department of Labor. *Projections 2000.* Bureau of Labor Statistics, Bulletin 2302, March, 1988. Available from Superintendent of Documents, U.S. Government Printing Office, Washington, D.C. 20402.

# NOTES

# NOTES

# NOTES

# NOTES

# OVER 150 BOOKS AND 35 VIDEOS AVAILABLE IN THE 50-MINUTE SERIES

**50-Minute Series Books and Videos Subject Areas . . .**

*Management*
*Training*
*Human Resources*
*Customer Service and Sales Training*
*Communications*
*Small Business and Financial Planning*
*Creativity*
*Personal Development*
*Wellness*
*Adult Literacy and Learning*
*Career, Retirement and Life Planning*

**Other titles available from Crisp Publications in these categories**

*Crisp Computer Series*
*The Crisp Small Business & Entrepreneurship Series*
*Quick Read Series*
*Management*
*Personal Development*
*Retirement Planning*